CREATING A POWERFUL Prayer MINISTRY IN YOUR CHURCH

Every Church Needs a Prayer Ministry

by Rev. Marilyn Burke Udeh

CREATING A POWERFUL Prayer MINISTRY IN YOUR CHURCH

Every Church Needs a Prayer Ministry

by Rev. Marilyn Burke Udeh

© 2021

Copyright © 2021
by Rev. Marilyn Burke Udeh

All rights reserved. No part of this book may be reprinted or reproduced in any form or by any electronic, mechanical, or other means, now known or hereafter invented, including photocopy, recording, and information storage and retrieval, without permission in writing from the publisher.

ISBN: 978-1-7346942-3-9
Library of Congress Control Number: 2021923251

Published by:
The Solid Foundation Group, LLC
Atlanta, Georgia
www.TheSolidFoundationGroup.com

Printed in the United States of America

Acknowledgements

I would like to extend my thanks and sincere appreciation to all who have contributed to the success of this publication.

First and foremost, I give honor and thanks to God Almighty who is my creator, my guide, my director, my leader, my advisor, my all and all for giving me the ability to write this book on *Creating A Prayer Ministry* for the world. Thanks be to God for the support and love shown to me. God has been mighty good, and I give Him all the praise and honor, in the name of Jesus.

Thanks to my husband, Bro. Sunday Christian Okechukwu Udeh, for always being by my side to lift me up with support in all my efforts; to my son, Bro. Alan Fitzgerald Johnson, who has always encouraged and supported me – walking and talking with me every step of the way about God's plan for our lives and the direction He has destined for our family members, and for providing information I may have needed in my movement along God's path.

Having started my ministry under the leadership of Rev. Dr. Jeffery B. Cooper who now serves as General Secretary/Chief Information Officer for the AME Church, I would like to take this opportunity to thank him for guiding me through my calling, providing wisdom and understanding of the process, and allowing me to preach, teach, lead, and serve under his tutelage. Although it was a difficult task starting out, I could always count on my senior pastor, Rev. Dr. Cooper, to lead me in the right direction. He was even there for me (and others) as we went through the Board of Examiners. In addition, I thank him for making sure I made the right educational choices to further my graduate studies in Divinity. I will forever be grateful for the instructions and leadership provided to me by Rev. Dr. J. B. Cooper.

For Rev. Vandy Simmons, I extend my sincere thanks for the leadership he provided during his tenure at Trinity AME Church. He assigned me the roles of Class Leader Coordinator, New Members' Coordinator, First Wednesday Night Session Coordinator, and Christian Education Director. I didn't know (at the time) the benefits of those appointments, but they assisted me tremendously in my classes at The Interdenominational Theological Center (ITC). Rev. Simmons provided suggestions, ideas, and served as a mentor as I studied at ITC and went through the Board of Examiners. Another great opportunity that was afforded me was leading First Wednesday Night Sessions. As a result of this opportunity, I gained so much from this role and from the sessions held on the first Wednesday of each month.

My former Pastor, Rev. Conitras Houston Dickens, whom we fondly called Pastor C., I'd like to reach forward to solemnly give thanks to her for allowing me to work alongside her as the Assistant Pastor of Trinity AME Church. I have learned more than I could have ever imagined from Pastor C., such as: leadership; teaching Bible Study at noon and in the evenings; working with the ministerial staff team members; working with the congregation in different aspects; going to serve communion to our sick and shut-in members; sitting in meetings with staff, trustees, stewards; church updates; official board meetings; church conferences; serving as Christian Education Director for the church; and leading as the Curriculum Director for the Trinity Early Learning Center. I will always be grateful to her for the leadership that comes with the position, the lessons learned as we teach the Word of God from the Holy Bible, her willingness to guide and lead me through the appointments, her attention to details as she teaches me the role as an assistant pastor in the field, understanding the importance of protocol in churches, and things to be mindful of as we walk the journey God has placed us on.

Thusly, on November 1, 2021, Trinity AME Church received our new Senior Pastor, Rev. Shawn Drains. Under the leadership of Rev. Drains, I am being guided to continue to serve as Assistant Pastor. With Rev. Drains at the helm, there are even additional opportunities for me to share my skills learned over the years and be a direct support to the ministry as an Assistant Pastor. Due to Rev. Drains' leadership style, Trinity is about to rise to higher heights spiritually.

Along my journey as a servant of God, I will never forget these four ministers who have influenced my life. Praise be to God for bringing those outstanding pastors my way.

I would also like to thank my Presiding Elder, Rev. Dr. David Rhone, Jr., for firing me up and encouraging me to move forward with a book that can be used for many years to come; Sis. Verline Moore, Bro. Bobby McVey, and Dr. Karen Armstrong for always being ready to assist me in any project that I may want to launch.

I appreciate each of you for all you have done to magnify God through me in my Christian walk with the Lord over these many years!

Dedication

This book is dedicated to every church in the United States of America and abroad to promote the creation of prayer ministries everywhere. When a church has a prayer ministry, it becomes a praying church, a fired-up church, a church where God resides, and its people know how to bend their knees and "have a little talk with the Lord." A praying church and its people are blessed by God, and God is truly in the prayer-answering business, hearing each and every prayer.

This Book is Presented to:

- Mr. Sunday Christian Okechukwu Udeh, *Husband*
- Mr. & Mrs. Alan Fitzgerald Johnson, *Son/Daughter-in-Law*
- Ms. Amari Johnson, Ms. Alana Johnson, and Ms. Heavenly Udeh, *Granddaughters*
- Mr. Brent Daniel, *Nephew*
- Ms. Felicia Banks, *Cousin/Daughter*

Table of Contents

Introduction 1

The Objectives 11

The Purpose 15

What Should Be Included in a Prayer? 19

Prayers for Different Occasions 27

- *A Prayer of Thanksgiving* 28
- *A Prayer for Forgiveness* 30
- *A Children's Prayer* 32
- *A Prayer for Health and Healing* 34
- *A Prayer for Unity* 36
- *A Prayer for Peace* 38
- *A Prayer of Praise* 40
- *A Prayer of Love* 41
- *A Prayer for Mental Illness* 42
- *A Prayer for a Pure Health and Wisdom* 44

Why Should We Pray? 47

The Power of Prayer 53

What Does it Take to Organize a
   Church Prayer Ministry? 59

Organizing A Church Prayer Ministry 63

What Is a Prayer Leader? 71

Summary 75

References 79

Introduction

This book was written to share the power of prayer and how establishing a relationship with God can lead us to where He wants us to be each day of our lives. To do this, however, we must allow God to use us daily for His purpose. We must know that God is willingly asking us to let go of our worries, let go of our ailments, let go of our trials and tribulations, and turn it all over to Him through corporate prayer. God is pleading with us to fall on our knees and pray to Him, for He is patiently waiting and listening to hear from each of us right now.

As I share my story of how this book came into existence, I hope that you, the reader, will view it as I do: An order from Almighty

God to fulfill His purpose. Allow this book to serve as a guide to start a prayer ministry in your church or virtually all over the world.

The thought of writing my first book came to mind while sitting in my Christian Education Class at the ITC. As a matter of fact, I had even given my first book a title: *From a Humble Beginning to the Call of God*. Later, while sitting in the coffee shop at ITC, I began to pull my thoughts together for my first book. Shortly thereafter, I became distracted with other things going on in life and never got my first book off the ground. After days, months, and years had passed, God spoke to me and said, "If you would have put as much time and energy into writing your book as you put into things, you would have finished writing your book by now." I thought to myself, "So true."

The next week in the Year 2020, I got a call from my Presiding Elder, Rev. Dr. David Rhone, Jr., discussing with me the plans as Christian Education Director for the South Atlanta District. He informed me that he was strongly interested in starting a prayer ministry in each church in the South Atlanta District. As we talked, the Presiding Elder, said to me, "You know people should be able to leave their knowledge and ideas behind as a guide for generations to come." Furthermore, he said, "As the Christian Education Director for the South Atlanta District, put something in the hands of the people. If they have something in their hands, they will have a guide. This was all motivating to me.

God's Word

For I know the plans I have for you, declares the Lord, plans to prosper you and not to harm you, plans to give you hope and a future.
~ Jeremiah 29:11

I thought the idea made great sense. As a matter of fact, he talked about a gentleman who was highly knowledgeable in the field of Christian Education, but who had passed away taking all that good information with him.

After he outlined all of my duties and responsibilities, I said, "WOW!" Then, God immediately spoke to me and said, "Take every opportunity to work hard and glorify me on a daily basis. You will be alright. I am your God. Just put your trust in me in whatever you do, and I will see you through. Obey my Word, and I will bless you. Do what I tell you to do and remember I have been there for you, always taking care of you, and I will continue to take care of you."

For some reason, I did not share my conversation with Presiding Elder Rhone, and the Presiding Elder did not know this conversation had already taken place between God and me at the center. I must confess that I did not know where God was leading me at the time; however, later, I realized that God's plan for me, first and foremost, was to organize a worldwide prayer ministry. What an amazing revelation! Bigger than I could have ever imagined!

The beauty of the prayer ministry is that is serves as a blueprint or instructional guide for individuals to create and organize successful prayer ministries throughout the United States of America as well as all over the world.

God's Word

And the peace of God, which transcends all understanding will guard your hearts and your minds in Christ Jesus.
~ Philippians 4:7

God reminds us that as we pray, He will be uplifted, praised, and glorified throughout the world. If you have a praying church, you will have a blessed church, and if you have a blessed church, you will have blessed people in the church. We must know the power of praying individually as well as the power of praying as a community.

I hope that this book will be the answer to many churches' prayers – that the information found within will help to organize successful prayer ministries and help churches realize the true power of prayer. The goal is to give members a prayer ministry that they can look forward to daily or weekly. A prayer leader makes the decision on how often the church will pray. We must ask God in prayer to intervene in our lives.

The more we pray, the more God answers our prayers, heals our sick and shut in, blesses our marriages, heals our land, saves sinners, and blesses us with more people praying. With more praying churches joining in for prayer, we will be able to build successful praying churches all over the world.

Through prayer, children and adults will be protected from all that is sinful and evil, lives will be changed and saved, employment will be obtained, prosperity will be gained, and so much more. There is power in prayer.

We know that where there are two or three gathered in the Name of God the Father, God is in the midst also, and God answers

---

God's Word

For the eyes of the Lord are on the righteous and his ears are attentive to their prayer, but the face of the Lord is against those who do evil.
~ 1 Peter 3:12

prayer. God has called us to call out to Him for whatever we want or need, and He answers. In the Book of Luke 18:1, God says:

> *This is the confidence we have in approaching God: that if we ask anything according to his will, he hears us.*

The vision that God gave me to write this book came back to me differently from my original plans to write a book. I believe God is saying, *"You wanted to write a book about your life's story much earlier, but I would not allow you to write that book at that time because I had another plan for your life. I wanted you to write this book for Me, which will glorify Me first. You will write a book about pulling My people together and helping them to understand the power of prayer. My people are wandering around all over the world with many problems, issues, and much frustration. They do not know to fall on their knees and call out to Me."*

God revealed this and is saying: *"People, you must pray, call out to me, ask me and it will be given unto you. Seek and you will find, knock and the door will be opened unto you. I will bless you through prayer. Prayer needs to start at the church and continue into every home. God is saying this: My churches must be in order and must be called a House of Prayer. You must complete My assignment before you write and publish the book you started some years ago."* God continued to say, *"Once you start writing your book, "Creating a Powerful Prayer Ministry," your book will be published."*

God's Word

*And call on me in the day of trouble;
I will deliver you, and you will honor me.
~ Psalm 50:15*

Rev. Marilyn Burke Udeh

I continued the Prayer Ministry Leadership role for the church's Prayer Ministry under the leadership of Rev. Conitras Houston Dickens (Pastor C). With the leadership of Pastor C, we have been able to move our Prayer Ministry forward and now, continuing under the leadership of Rev. Shawn Drains.

Currently, our prayer ministry meets once per week and includes the following: 1) an opening prayer; 2) a brief biblical lesson where we all are encouraged to participate (giving all attendees an opportunity to share their thoughts with the group); 3) a request for prayer and praise reports; 4) an ending short motivational message; and 5) a closing prayer. This session is completed within 60 minutes every Thursday of each week.

During Lent 2021, and Women's History Month, we utilized our Thursday Prayer Session to include a child (age 9) by the name of Little Sis. Casey Williams (from our Young People's Department), along with young adult members of our ministerial team, and our senior-prayer warriors to pray. After the biblical lesson, we prayed, and finally, had a closing motivational word. A great time in the Lord in only one hour.

As quoted by E.M. Bounds, without prayer, "the church becomes a graveyard, not an army equipped for battle. Praise and prayer are stifled, and worship is dead." If there is not a praying church, the church is lost and will not be able to develop soldiers for the Battlefield ahead and within. We must pray, so we will all be

---

God's Word

For everyone who asks receives; the one who seeks finds; and to the one who knocks, the door will be opened.
~ Matthew 7:8

equipped as soldiers to be ready for battle – whatever the battle may be in our lives.

When we are faced with sinful deeds, the battle comes. Are we ready for battle? When we are confronted with issues of life, are we ready for battle? When we are asking God to turn lives around, are we ready for battle?

We must be ready through sincere prayer to God. Pray and pray continually as it is stated in the Bible,

> *1 Thessalonians 5:16-18 NIV - Rejoice always, pray continually, give thanks in all circumstances; for this is God's will for you in Christ Jesus.*

We've got to pray and pray sincerely to God because God answers prayer. With that being said, we must pray.

We must make prayer a daily part of our lives and be ready for our weekly prayer through our churches. Include as many people as possible in your weekly prayer session. Just know that where two or three are gathered in the mighty name of God, God will be right there in the midst, as well. If you start with two or three people, just know that God is right there with you. Try to include a child or children, and young adults, as well, so that they will not be afraid or ashamed to pray in public. Train up a child in the direction he or she is to go, and the child will not depart from those teachings.

God's Word

*You will pray to him, and he will hear you,
and you will fulfill your vows.*
~ Job 22:27

Start your prayer ministry, regardless of the number of people who participates. If it is small, thank God and start small and let God grow the ministry. If it is mediocre, thank God, start the ministry and you will see the blessings of God. If it is large, we thank God and move forward with the number of individuals who have heard the call of God.

As the ministry grows, you will be able to organize the ministry into different Prayer Ministries, such as a Children's Prayer Ministry, the Young Adults' Prayer Ministry, the Adults' Prayer Ministry, and/or a Seniors' Prayer Ministry.

In the event you are not ready to have the different groups break away into individual sessions according to age, then keep them all together. The leader should allow God to direct the path as to whether to stay together or to break into individual groups. Pray and offer up a prayer to God for the church, for peace, for sickness, for strength, for love, for neighbors, for justice, for our virtual audience, for our young people, and for world peace. Let God use the people for God's glory.

Praying is very important to the life of our people and to the life of the church. As a result of working with my Presiding Elder, Rev. Dr. Rhone, Jr., I had to turn around and reorganize my church prayer ministry to reflect the mission for the South Atlanta District of the AME Church's Prayer Ministry. The goal is to create a prayer ministry to reflect the lessons God taught us and the model Jesus used to teach his disciples to prayer. There is more power when

---

God's Word

And they continued stedfastly in the apostles' doctrine and fellowship, and in breaking of bread, and in prayers.
~ Acts 2:42

we have two or three people gathered in prayer with the same intent and focus. The Bible says, *"For where two or three are gathered together in my name, there am I in the midst of them (Matthew 18:20 KJV)."*

As we pray, we must develop that feeling to let go of our troubles and give it all to the Lord in our prayer.

If you would work to get the people accustomed to praying daily and with a group prayer at the end of the week, the people will understand the power of prayer, the people will be able to witness the power of prayer, and the people will understand to call on the Lord with all their hearts and with all their strength.

God is a prayer-answering God when our prayers are aligned with God's plans for our lives.

God's Word

The Lord is far from the wicked, but he hears the prayer of the righteous.
~ Proverbs 15:29

The Objectives

The goal is to establish an effective prayer ministry in your church to meet the needs of all of God's people or a prayer ministry that the people can call out to God for prayer. Any time made for prayer is always a good thing and a great opportunity to connect with God. He is waiting for you to come to Him, so you will know that He is all you need.

God does not want us to wait to pray. Just pray, and talk with Him at any time – morning, noon, or night. Pray anywhere, even while swimming, driving, walking, talking, working, before eating, before going to bed, while in the bed, and when we rise in the morning.

God has commanded us in God's Word to pray as stated in:

> *Philippians 4:6-7 – Don't worry about anything; instead, pray about everything. Tell God what you need, and thank him for all he has done. Then you will experience God's peace, which exceeds anything we can understand. His peace will guard your heart and minds as you live in Christ Jesus.*

It is so amazing that God has given each of us an awesome weapon to use against our adversaries – Prayer. To activate that weapon, all we have to do is fall on our knees and pray out to God. God will answer prayer in due time. That timing may not be the time we are expecting; but, rest assured the answer to our prayers will always be right on time and a time that is just right for us. There is an old saying, "God may not answer when we want God to answer, but the answer will be right on time."

I am a living witness to that statement because I have prayed so much that I thought God was not going to answer my prayers; but, God did answer my prayers and at the right time.

There are five objectives we must aim to accomplish our goals of having a Powerful Prayer Ministry. These objectives will help you organize a successful prayer ministry at your church:

1. Build a Prayer Ministry as commanded by God.

God's Word

Pray then like this: "Our Father in heaven, hallowed be your name. Your kingdom come, your will be done, on earth as it is in heaven. Give us this day our daily bread, and forgive us our debts, as we also have forgiven our debtors. And lead us not into temptation but deliver us from evil.
~ Matthew 6:9-13

Acts 6:4 – But we will give ourselves continually to prayer, and to the ministry of the word.

Luke 18:1 - Then Jesus told his disciples a parable to show them that they should always pray and not give up.

2. **Define the Power of Prayer so each person will know why the prayer ministry is so important.**

   Psalm 107:28-30 – Then they cried to the Lord in their trouble, and he delivered them from their distress; he made the storm be still, and the waves of the sea were hushed. Then they were glad because they had quiet, and he brought them to their desired haven.

   Matthew 21:22 – Whatever you ask for in prayer in faith, you will receive.

3. **Develop a Prayer Ministry for different groups in the church.**

   I Timothy 2:1-4 – First of all, then, I urge that supplication, prayers, intercessions, and thanksgiving be made for everyone, for kings and all who are in high positions, so that we may lead a quiet and peaceable life in all godliness and dignity. This is right and is acceptable in the sight of God

---

God's Word

Then they cried to the LORD in their trouble, and he delivered them from their distress. He made the storm be still, and the waves of the sea were hushed. Then they were glad that the waters were quiet, and he brought them to their desired haven.
~ Psalm 107:28-30

our Savior, who desires everyone to be saved and to come to the knowledge of the truth.

Ephesians 6:18 – Pray in the Spirit at all times in every prayer and supplication. To that end keep alert and always persevere in supplication for all the saints.

4. **Designate a Prayer Leader with a Team of Prayer Warriors.**

    1 John 5:14-15 – And this is the boldness we have in him, that if we ask anything according to his will, he hears us. And if we know that we know that he hears us in whatever we ask, we know that we have obtained the requests made of him.

    Isaiah 65:24 – Before they call I will answer, while they are yet speaking I will hear.

5. **Establish and agree upon a day or days of the week, time, and place for the prayer session.**

    Thessalonians 5:17 – Pray without ceasing

    Luke 18:1 – Then Jesus told them a parable about their need to pray always and not to lose heart.

Once the five objectives have been mastered, your prayer ministry will be ready to take off.

God's Word

"Call to me and I will answer you and tell you great and unsearchable things you do not know."
~ Jeremiah 33:3

The Purpose

There is a major purpose behind establishing a Prayer Ministry or Ministries in every church – God answers prayers.

God is available to every one of his children and is available at our beckoning call. All we have to do is call out to God Almighty who is a prayer-answering God.

To establish praying churches all over the world, it is very important for each church to establish a Prayer Ministry that includes the youth, teenagers, young adults, adults, and seniors. We want praying to become a part of all our members. As the young become adults and then seniors, the practice will already be a part of their lives. Training the child at an early age in the way of the Lord our God will result in that child not departing from the teachings. Children will not allow the devil to overtake their lives, and this is a great lesson to learn at an early age. This prayer time should include members of the church, non-members of the church, families, neighbors, co-workers, and friends. Bring all the people together or invite them to join you for prayer in person or online.

Once the people feel that the prayer ministry is open to every person, the people will feel a sense of belonging and will welcome others to participate. Start your prayer ministry and include all of God's children. The more people you invite, the more people you will have learning to pray and feeling comfortable about praying.

God brings great change in our lives when prayer is the catalyst. The boring and dead condition or the need for an egocentric performance in the church simply reflects an ineffective and weak prayer life. We need powerful times of prayer, devotion, and worship. As stated by Al Whittinghill, "Without the heartbeat of prayer, the body of Christ will resemble a corpse. The church is dying on her feet because she is not living on her knees."

Jesus has instructed us on how to pray, giving us a model in which to use. This model prayer is included in this book, along with prayers for different occasions.

Forming and assembling the different groups for prayer, the church, then, becomes a house of prayer. A house of prayer is established when we can get the church praying regularly to God

God's Word

Now this I know: The Lord gives victory to his anointed. He answers him from his heavenly sanctuary with the victorious power of his right hand.
~ Psalm 20:6

for the many situations, blessings, and struggles of life. We are all confronted with life's burdens and must call upon God Almighty for help. When we call upon the Lord for help, we learn to lean upon the Lord for every need in our life.

The people should gather for the purpose of prayer for all the issues they have been confronted with in their lives; and all God's children will be blessed. If it is a virtual climate, then the same thing will take place as we pray from our personal dwellings.

God's Word

Answer me when I call to you, my righteous God.
Give me relief from my distress; have
mercy on me and hear my prayer.
~ Psalm 4:1

What Should Be Included in a Prayer?

When we pray, we should be sure to acknowledge God – first – for who He is, Praise Him in Love for all He has done for us, give Him thanks for all He has done for us, be bold and admit our sins to Him. We should also pray for others and repent of our own sins by letting God know that we are sorry for our past mistakes and/or conduct. We should ask God for forgiveness, submit all power to

God, and finally, ask God to help us be the person He wants us to be. This is our prayer. In the Mighty Name of Jesus, the Christ, we pray. Amen, Amen, Amen!

Listed below are the ten essential elements to having a powerful prayer, as instructed by Professor Cynthia Rivers (ITC).

Acknowledgement
To regard or describe God's Deity as our God or to recognize Him as genuine. A call on God's omniscient, omnipotent, and omnipresence power.

Adoration/Praise
Worship given to God alone or a feeling of profound love and admiration. Glorify God and give accolades in celebrating our God.

Thanksgiving
Give thanks for the blessings. Give thanks to the God Almighty.

Confession
An admission of misdeeds or fault. Admitting our sins.

Petition
A time to pray for your personal needs.
Your personal request to God.

God's Word

*Whoever gives heed to instruction prospers,
and blessed is the one who trusts in the Lord
~ Proverbs 16:20*

Repentance
   Remorse for your past conduct. Vowing to never commit that past sin again.

Forgiveness
   Compassionate feelings that support a willingness to forgive. Forgiving for an act and thought of doing harm to others.

Intercession
   A prayer to God on behalf of another person. Intervene on behalf of another.

Submission
   Surrendering your whole life to God. Keeping promises made to God.

Ascription
   Assigning some quality or character to God. Acknowledgement of who your prayer is ascribed to or prayed to.

As we pray using the factors listed above, we want to make sure that we are fully aware of each word and its meaning. Pay close attention to what you are saying to God and mean it from the bottom of your heart.

Although there are ten elements listed above, every prayer doesn't have to include all elements to be a powerful prayer. According to scripture Peter called out to Jesus and Jesus said, "Take courage! It

God's Word

*Be joyful in hope, patient in affliction,
faithful in prayer.
~ Romans 12:12*

is I. Don't be afraid." Then Peter said, "Lord, if it's you, tell me to come to you on the water." Jesus responded, "Come!" Then Peter got down out of the boat, walked on the water and came toward Jesus. But when he saw the wind, he was afraid and, beginning to sink, cried out, "Lord, save me!" Immediately Jesus reached out his hand and caught him. "You of little faith," he said, "why did you doubt?" And when they climbed into the boat, the wind died down. Then those who were in the boat worshiped him, saying, "Truly you are the Son of God." (Matthew 14:27-33). This was Peter's prayer to God and God answered his prayer. Sometimes a prayer as short as "Lord, save me!" is all that is needed. Praise God.

The following are two prayers showing how each of the above elements are used:

(1)

Acknowledgement
Almighty and everlasting God, how majestic is Your name in all the earth! We acknowledge Your glory of the eternal Trinity, and we magnify Your Holy Name.

Adoration/Praise
Oh, Holy Spirit. You gave Your only begotten son that we may live again, and for that we glorify Your Holy Name. You are worthy to be praised.

God's Word

In all your ways acknowledge Him,
And He shall direct your paths.
~ Proverbs 3:6

Thanksgiving
Spirit of the Living God, You sit on Your throne as our eternal Lord, and we thank You for all Your blessings.

Confession
Everlasting and creator, God, I confess that I have not been the person you have destined, nor have I walked the path you have prepared for me. Help me, Oh God, to stay on the path you have already destined for my life.

Petition
Our eternal, omnipotent God, please cleanse our hearts, wipe our slates clean, and help us to keep our minds on You throughout this worship service.

Repentance
Holy Spirit, we repent for our failure to acknowledge You in all that we do and for our wicked ways exhibited toward your people.

Forgiveness
Most merciful God, please forgive us right now in the name of Jesus for all our sins committed – known and unknown.

Intercession
Oh, Holy Spirit, protect us from all that is sinful and evil. God, please bless those individuals who are homeless and without food.

God's Word
And if we know that he hears us – whatever we ask – we know that we have what we asked of him.
~ 1 John 5:15

Submission
Prepare us for this worship experience by bringing our hearts and minds back to You.

Ascription
This is our prayer, oh Holy Spirit, and we ask You to please hear our prayer this day in the matchless name of Jesus Christ, our Lord and Savior. Amen, Amen, and Amen!

(2)
The All-Inclusive Prayer: **THE LORD'S PRAYER**

Acknowledgement
Our Father, which art in heaven,

Adoration/Praise
Hallowed be thy Name.

Petition
Thy kingdom come. Let thy will be done on earth as it is in heaven. Give us this day our daily bread.

Confession/Repentance
And forgive us our trespasses,

Forgiveness
as we forgive them that trespass again us.

God's Word

Repent, then, and turn to God, so that your sins may be wiped out, that times of refreshing may come from the Lord.
~ Acts 3:19

Intercession
Lead us not into temptation,

Submission
but deliver us from evil.

Ascription
For thine is the kingdom, the power, and the glory for ever and ever. Amen!

God's Word

Brothers and sisters, pray for us.
~ I Thessalonians 5:25

Prayers for Different Occasions

The following pages include 10 different prayers
in which you may use to pray at any time.

A Prayer of Thanksgiving

Almighty God, You are the maker of Heaven and Earth, and we thank You for this day. We thank You for walking and talking with us each day of our lives.

Dear God, we come before You right now with thanksgiving in our hearts for all You have done for us over the many years of our lives. God, You have been good to us and for that we thank You. We thank You for family and friends. We thank You for walking with us and talking with us. We thank You for this day, God, and for all your blessings.

Almighty God, let us enter Your gates with thanksgiving and into Your courts with praise. We just can't thank You enough, even if we had multiple tongues. Your Grace and Your mercy have been with us, and for that we just want to raise our voices and thank You.

Oh, Holy God, we have not been the persons You want us to be; but, God, we ask You for your forgiveness. Most Holy God, help

God's Word

Let us come before His presence with thanksgiving;
Let us shout joyfully to Him with psalms, for the Lord
is the great God, and the great King above all gods.
~ Psalms 95:2-3

us to not fall into temptation. Help us to resist the devil and walk in Your ways.

Most merciful God, work with us and help us to be the persons you have designed us to be. We have strayed away from You, and we are asking You to bring us on back to You, dear God, and to Your will. This is our prayer in the mighty name of Jesus, we pray. Amen.

God's Word

Do not be anxious about anything, but in every situation, by prayer and petition, with thanksgiving, present your requests to God.
~ Philippians 4:6

A Prayer for Forgiveness

Dear Heavenly Father, we come giving You all the honor and all the glory, for You are a mighty good God. And, for that we just want to say, thank You.

We ask You, Dear God, to have mercy upon us, our families and friends, and to grant us Your peace. We come to You right now, in the name of Jesus, to just say thank You. Holy, Holy One, we come in Your presence with joy in our hearts for being a mighty good God. Oh, Holy One, blot out our sins and transgressions and wash us clean from all our iniquities…and clean us up – right now – so, we will be able to walk right with You.

Dear God, Dear God, we acknowledge our transgressions and our sinful nature. Clean us up, Oh Lord. We ask You, because You have the power to do so, and for that we are truly grateful. Make us to know Your joy. Make us to know Your peace. Make us to know Your love. Make us to know You are right with us and will never leave us nor will you ever forsake us.

God's Word

If my people, who are called by my name, will humble themselves and pray and seek my face and turn from their wicked ways, then I will hear from heaven, and I will forgive their sin and will heal their land.
~ 2 Chronicles 7:14

Keep us out of the devil's path. Keep us away from all that is sinful and evil. Keep us away from confusion. And, God, we will give You all the honor and all the praise. Keep us in Your safety for the rest of our lives.

Forgive us for not forgetting those who have wronged us, who have spoken against us, and for the bitterness we have harbored in our hearts. Dear God, please forgive us for the anger we could not shake off or forget. Forgive us for the resentment in our spirit. Dear God, forgive us right now in the name of Jesus. Amen.

God's Word

*The LORD is near to all who call on him,
to all who call on him in truth. He fulfills
the desires of those who fear him; he
hears their cry and saves them.*
~ Psalm 145:18-19

A Children's Prayer

Almighty God, You are the creator of Heaven and Earth and for that we thank You. You are *our* creator and for that we also say thank You, Dear God. God, we thank you for waking us up this morning and for allowing us to attend school virtually, home trained, or in person. We thank you for the opportunity to learn day by day, and to be the person You want us to be…to live the way You want us to live…and to serve You the way You want us to serve.

God, You have been good to us, and You already know what we need, even before we ask You, Dear God. Oh, Merciful God, bless all the children in Your own special way.

Dear Holy God, forgive us, our family members, and all our buddies and friends from all our evil and sinful ways. Forgive us for all our sins. Forgive us for anyone we might have hurt or did not forgive. Almighty and everlasting God, forgive us for not helping our friends when they needed us. God, You are a mighty good God and for that we thank You.

God's Word

I pray that the eyes of your heart may be enlightened in order that you may know the hope to which he has called you, the riches of his glorious inheritance in his holy people.
~ Ephesians 1:18

Thank You for leading us and guiding us in the path You have already laid out for us. Help us, our friends, and our families to love each other as You have told us to do. God, teach us Your ways, so we all can go to Heaven and live with You there forevermore. God, no matter what comes our way, teach us to come to You in prayer for direction, for comfort, for peace, and for Your love.

Help the adults to know that we are trying and help them to lead us in the right direction. Help us to learn Your words, Your ways, and Your love, so we can live like You want us to live.

Dear God keep our parents, sisters, brothers, teachers, friends, classmates, family members, principals, school staff members, all our cousins, our frog, our goldfish, and our cat safe in this sin sick world. God, also keep our doctors, all the healthcare workers, our pastor, our church family, the firemen, the policemen, the ambulance workers, and everyone we know in your awesome care. Help us to be able to complete great projects and lead our classmates, our buddies, friends, and others in the path You have set for them. This is our prayer. In the mighty name of Jesus. we pray. Amen.

God's Word

I prayed for this child, and the Lord
has granted me what I asked of him.
~ 1 Samuel 1:27

A Prayer for Health and Healing

Dear Holy God, we are Your creation. You are the Holy One, and for that we love You, Dear God. You are a just God, a loving God, and a merciful God. For that we thank You, most merciful God.

Heavenly Father, continue to lead us and guide us to be the persons You want us to be. Thank You for being right by our sides, protecting us every step of the way on a daily basis.

Most merciful God, we call upon Your Holy Name for a blessing of restored good health and a blessing of healing right now, in the name of Jesus. God, You are good and God, You are able to do what You said You would do. Bless us all and our family members, too.

Most Holy God, forgive us of our sins and lead us in the path You have designed for us. Forgive us for not repenting of our sins, for not acknowledging our wrongdoings, and for not forgiving others who have not walked in the path you have laid out for them. Forgive us for all our sins and grant us Your love. God, grant us Your love, Your peace, and Your comfort.

God's Word

"But I will restore you to health and heal your wounds,' declares the LORD"

~ Jeremiah 30:17

Protect us right now from all of Satan's evil schemes. Clean us up, oh God, from the spirit of evil leaders. Oh, God, please allow Your people to move forward and not be destroyed by the evil deeds of others. God, right now, in the name of Jesus, we need Your divine protection. Let no weapon formed against us prosper. God, we call upon Your name for a complete restoration of healing. God, You are able, and You have the power to restore great health, to restore a healing to our bodies, and to help us rise from our sick bed to do your will.

God, walk with us, walk with the doctors who are treating your people, and talk with us for encouragement. Give us the knowledge and the ability to pray continually for Your healing powers. Where we are weak, lift us up. Where our rest is broken, give us an opportunity to sleep peacefully. Restore our bodies so we can heal and perform healing techniques on your people. Heal our bodies right now, Dear God.

God, release Your miraculous power upon Your people for a complete healing. God, we know that You do have the power to heal and restore. Help us, God, to be the persons you want us to be and God, we will give You all the honor, and all the power. In the mighty name of Jesus, we pray, Amen.

God's Word

My prayer is not that you take them out of the world but that you protect them from the evil one.
~ John 17:15

A Prayer for Unity

Dear Loving God, we come before You on this day to praise Your Holy Name, to give You thanks, and to worship You. You are a mighty good God, a loving God, a caring God, a just God, a protecting God, a healer, and a rock in a weary land. God, You are awesome and for that we give You all the honor, all the praise, and all the glory, for You are worthy to be praised.

God, we ask You right now, in the name of Jesus, for unity among Your people, that we may work together for the good of all Your people.

Heavenly Father, forgive us for not forgiving others. Forgive us for all our sins. Forgive us for not working daily for peace and love amongst your people. God, grant us Your love, Your wisdom, and Your understanding each day of our lives.

God, cleanse us from the top of our heads to the bottom of our feet, so we will live right according to Your plan, and to do right towards our neighbors, and to treat others the way You want us to live daily. Help us to walk in the path You have destined for us.

God's Word

*And over all these virtues put on love,
which binds them all together
in perfect unity.*
~ Colossians 3:14

Help us to speak Your words to others, so that they may grow closer to You. Dear God, help us to be just in all that we do. Work with us, Dear God. Work with us. This is our prayer. In the mighty name of Jesus, we pray. Amen.

God's Word

Finally, all of you, be like-minded, be sympathetic, love one another, be compassionate and humble.

~ 1 Peter 3:8

A Prayer for Peace

Dear Heavenly Father, we come to You this day as humble as we know how praising Your Holy Name, worshipping You, and giving You all the honor and all the praise – for You are a mighty good God; and, for that, we thank You, in the mighty name of Jesus.

We come to you on bended knees to thank You, to praise You and to honor Your Holy Name. We thank You for Your blessings upon our lives. God, we thank You for always being there for us in all that we do in the mighty name of Jesus Christ.

Spirit of the Living God, fall afresh on us this day as we pray for peace throughout the world. God, we call upon You, because we need You to create peace in a sin-sick world that has lost touch with You. So, God, we call upon You right now, in the Name of Jesus, for Your Peace to rain down like a mighty flood upon Your people. God, you are able to bring peace and we call upon Your Holy Name for a healing of peace on the land.

God, please forgive us of all our sins. Dear Holy One, we call upon Your name for a cleansing from all those sinful thoughts, those sinful ideas, sinful nature toward mankind, and those sinful deeds. Please gracious God, cleanse our minds to be able to forgo all that is sinful and live the lives You have planned for us.

God's Word

If any of you lacks wisdom, you should ask God, who gives generously to all without finding fault, and it will be given to you.
~ James 1:5

Help us to be a way maker, to create peace among Your people wherever we go. God, please go with us from day to day. In Jesus' name, we pray. Amen.

God's Word

"Peace I leave with you, My peace I give to you; not as the world gives do I give to you. Let not your heart be troubled, neither let it be afraid."
~ John 14:27

A Prayer of Praise

Dear Merciful God, we thank You for Your many blessings bestowed upon each of us daily. Thank You for being our guide and for remaining with us each day of our lives.

Most precious God, we praise You, we lift Your Holy Name up high, and we give You all of the honor and praise. Most Holy God, we have not been the people we should have been, and we ask for Your forgiveness. God, You know we have not followed Your plan and for that we are asking You to forgive us. Forgive us of all our sins and keep us from falling into sinful situations day by day. God, when You lead us, help us to be able to stay on the right track of life.

Dear God, we ask that You clean us up, so You can use us in a mighty way. God, You are able to create in us a clean heart and renew a right spirit within us. God, You can keep us from falling when we are stricken with the anxieties of the world.

God, You have been good to us. You have walked with us and talked with us in all that we do. Prepare us for Your work. Prepare us for Your will. Prepare us for Your service and prepare us to be the little light that shines in dark places. This is our prayer in the mighty name of Jesus Christ. Amen!

God's Word

Is anyone among you in trouble? Let them pray.
Is anyone happy? Let them sing songs of praise.
~ James 5:13

A Prayer of Love

Dear God, you are the answer to all our situations. You are holy indeed. You are mighty in power. You are our only God on this earth. We praise your Holy Name, and we give you all our love, glory, and honor.

God, we thank You for this day as we show You our love and as we display Your love amongst Your people. God, bless us and keep us as we fulfill Your will. Help us to love those who have despitefully used us, who have talked about us maliciously, and who have sinned against us. God, You said in Your Word,

> *You shall love the Lord your God with all your heart and with all your soul and with all your mind. This is the great and first commandment. And a second is like it: You shall love your neighbor as yourself. (Matthew 22:36-40).*

Oh, Holy One, Our God, deliver us all from evil and keep us as Your good, decent, and humble servants. This is our prayer. In the mighty name of Jesus. Amen!!

God's Word

"But to you who are listening I say: Love your enemies, do good to those who hate you, bless those who curse you, pray for those who mistreat you.
~ Luke 6:27-28

A Prayer for Mental Illness

Our God, the creator of Heaven and Earth, we come before You giving You all the praise and all the honor. God, we thank you for being God all by Yourself – mighty and powerful. God, You are the ruler over every man on this earth. God, we ask You to keep us in all that we do. Stay with us and protect us.

Most Merciful God, we thank You for being a loving God, a God of forgiveness, a God who will wipe away our sins, and a God who is a protector for Your children. We thank You, God, for always being with us. God, you have never left us nor forsaken us, for it was us who left your side, and for that, God, we give You all the glory and all the praise.

God, we have not been what we should have been, nor have we done what we should have done; but, God, we ask You for a healing from mental illness.

Most Merciful God, provide the right help we need to help clear up mental illness amongst your people. Search us out, Oh Lord, for the help that is needed for lives to be saved, for relationships

God's Word

You desire but do not have, so you kill. You covet but you cannot get what you want, so you quarrel and fight. You do not have because you do not ask God.
~ James 4:2

to be corrected and mended, for peace from the illness, and protection from the illness. God, You are able to rescue Your people from the destruction this illness brings.

Forgive us of our sins and keep us in Your safety. Deliver us from all that is sinful and evil. God, you know all about our trials and tribulations. Keep us free from the devil and bless each and every one of us. In the mighty name of Jesus, the Christ, we pray. Amen.

God's Word

Therefore confess your sins to each other and pray for each other so that you may be healed. The prayer of a righteous person is powerful and effective.
~ James 5:16

A Prayer for a Pure Heart and Wisdom

Almighty God, You are our creator, and You are the maker of Heaven and Earth. God, we give You praise and honor for life and Your blessings upon us. God, You have been good to each of us and for that we thank You wholeheartedly.

Holy God, we thank You for all You have done for us, provided for us, and for all the love You have shown to us. We thank You for watching over us day and night.

Forgive us of our sins. Forgive us for not forgiving our neighbors and help us to walk in Your ways – morning, noon, and night.

Most Gracious and Holy God, do not let us fall into temptation. Keep us lifted to do Your will with the right spirit within us. Bless us, Dear God, with a clean heart, a pure heart…and with Your Godly wisdom. Do not take your wisdom away from us. Do not let us be blinded from Your truths. And help us to teach our sons and daughters from generations to generations your wisdom, and Lord, help us develop a pure heart.

God's Word

For there is no difference between Jew and Gentile—the same Lord is Lord of all and richly blesses all who call on him, for, "Everyone who calls on the name of the Lord will be saved."
~ Romans 10:12-13

God, we've got more work to do for You and more praises to lift up to You, Dear God. Keep us, protect us, and help us to love with a pure and genuine heart. In the name of Jesus, we pray. Amen!!!!

God's Word

Therefore everyone who hears these words of mine and puts them into practice is like a wise man who built his house on the rock.
~ Matthew 7:24

Why Should We Pray?

The Bible commands us to pray and it is found in scripture throughout the Bible to *pray and to pray continually, giving thanks in all circumstances, for this is God's will for you in Christ Jesus, 1 Thessalonians 5:17-18*.

In the Bible, Jesus prayed to God on many different occasions. If Jesus prayed, then we surely should pray for all that ails us, from joyous times to sad times, from weaknesses to strongholds that we may endure to the end, from sicknesses to healings, from asking for help to getting assistance, from falling into temptation to standing up against the evils of life, from bad to good, from going in the wrong direction to a major change. God is able to answer prayers.

Furthermore, God has commanded us to pray according to scriptures. Just to list five of the many scriptures found in the Bible about prayer, Jesus said:

> *"Watch and pray so that you will not fall into temptation. The spirit is willing, but the flesh is weak." (Matthew 26:41)*

> *"It is written," he said to them, "My house will be called a house of prayer, but you are making it a den of robbers". (Matthew 21:13)*

> *"Do not be anxious about anything, but in every situation, by prayer and petition, with thanksgiving, present your requests to God. And the peace of God, which surpasses all understanding, will guard your hearts and your minds in Christ Jesus." (Philippians 4:6-7)*

> *"This, then, is how you should pray: 'Our Father in heaven, hallowed be your name, your kingdom come, your will be done, on earth as it is in heaven. Give us today our daily bread. And forgive us our debts, as we also have forgiven our debtors. And lead us not into temptation, but deliver us from the evil one.' (Matthew 6:9-13)*

God's Word

I call on you, my God, for you will answer me;
turn your ear to me and hear my prayer.
~ Psalm 17:6

> *But I tell you, love your enemies and pray for those who persecute you (Matthew 5:44)*

We pray because it is how we communicate with God, and it is how we ask God for what we want on a daily basis. Jesus taught his disciples to pray, and he used the Lord's Prayer as a model prayer for God's children to follow. It is an inclusive prayer. See it below:

> *The Lord's Prayer:*
> *Our Father, which art in heaven, Hallowed be thy Name. They Kingdom come. Let thou will be done on earth as it is in heaven. Give us this day our daily bread. And forgive us our trespasses, as we forgive them that trespass again us. Lead us not into temptation, but deliver us from evil. For thine is the kingdom, the power, and the glory for ever and ever. Amen!*

Prayer is our way of connecting with God and asking God for what we want in the Name of Jesus Christ. One of the most important things in our life is found in the power of Prayer. Prayer is the most important thing we can learn to do in our lives.

With the Word of God and through prayer, we are left with a plan to live a successful, fun, peaceful, and loving life. Jesus said,

---

God's Word

Therefore I want the men everywhere to pray, lifting up holy hands without anger or disputing.
~ 1 Timothy 2:8

> *"Ask and it will be given to you; seek and you will find; knock and the door will be opened to you. For everyone who ask receives; and to him who knocks, the door will be opened"* (Matthew 7:9).

We have desires, needs, and wants in life and God has given us the vehicle to receive what He has for us – Prayer.

We pray for God to heal us and our neighbors, the sick and shut-in, and family members and friends. We pray to reach a goal that is destined by God for us to reach. We pray for God to bless us. We pray for different needs, and we pray for peace among the people. With people, there are many reasons to pray, as we'll need God to intervene in our lives. We must call on God if we want our situations resolved.

Through prayer, we learn to talk with God, connect with God, make improvements in our lives, reach the goals God has for us, and ask for God's guidance. We pray for God to lead us, to speak for us, to talk to us, and for God to use us every day of our lives. This request to God can be all in one prayer, many times, over and over again. Praying until God does something. We should never fail to let God take our trials because we cannot reach the desired outcome without God.

We talk to God through prayer, and we receive God's blessings right before our eyes daily. God takes care of His children when we live an obedient life according to God's commands. God is a

---

God's Word

If you, then, though you are evil, know how to give good gifts to your children, how much more will your Father in heaven give good gifts to those who ask him!
~ Matthew 7:11

prayer-answering God and God will answer our prayers in His perfect timing. The Bible says,

> "Be Still and know that I am God; God will be exalted among the nations, God will be exalted in the earth." (Psalm 46:10).

It is so amazing to witness the Holy Spirit at work through prayer. As we pray, God answers prayer, and you know God is with us in all that we do. All we must do is hold on to God's unchanging hand, place your trust in God, and leave it with the Lord.

Pray because prayer works. It works for me, and it will work for you, too. Never, ever doubt what prayer can do for you, never doubt what prayer can do for the world, and never doubt what prayer can do for God's people. God has given us a precious gift to call upon Him and He will answer our prayers.

With the power of prayer, we do not have to worry about anything because God has said in His word as listed in scripture below:

> *Do not be anxious about anything, but in every situation, by prayer and petition, with thanksgiving, present your requests to God. And the peace of God, which transcends all understanding, will guard your hearts and your minds in Christ Jesus. (Philippians 4:6-7)*

God's Word

Now my eyes will be open and my ears attentive to the prayers offered in this place.
~ 2 Chronicles 7:15

The Power of Prayer

Prayer is Powerful!!!!

I am a living witness to the power of Prayer. At this point, I would like to share a couple of testimonies about the power of prayer.

Due to the fact that my father was very ill, he had been admitted into the hospital. I went to visit him and after a few hours had passed, I was told that visiting hours were up for the Intensive Care Unit (ICU). Instead of going home, God led me to go downstairs to the waiting room. While in the waiting room, I took out papers I had brought to grade. While grading the papers, I kept hearing different codes being called over the P.A. (Public Announcement) System. God allowed me to recall the Code Blue for some reason.

A lady sitting in the waiting room said to me, "They are surely calling a lot of codes today." I responded, "Do not worry, they call codes all the time around here." Shortly thereafter, I got a call on my cell phone. It was one of my father's nurses asking, "Are you still in the hospital?" I replied, "Yes." She then asked, "Will you please come up to your father's room?" Again, my response was, "Yes."

As I approached the floor of my father's room, there were approximately eight to 10 nurses and doctors at the door to his room. I quickly approached the room, having no earthly idea what was going on. One doctor said to me, "We just lost your father and we are so very sorry about your loss." My response was, "My loss? What?" "Mrs. Udeh, your father has passed." "Passed? Sir, I do not understand what you are talking about because I just left my father! At the time I left him, he was stable and that could not have been the end for him." I immediately stated, "Wherever he went, I need for you all to bring him back." One doctor responded, "Let's go to work", meaning cardiopulmonary resuscitation.

They quickly went into rescue mode. While they were working, I stood on a chair and just called on the Name of the Lord, my God!

God's Word

This is the confidence we have in approaching God: that if we ask anything according to his will, he hears us.
~ *1 John 5:14*

"Oh, God, I need You right now, in the Mighty Name of Jesus I pray. God, please bring my father back. I am praying to You right now, God. You are a prayer-answering God and I need for you to bring my father back to earth. I need you right now to answer my prayer. Please, God!"

I prayed on and on asking God to return my father. My call on God was getting louder and louder. By this time, I had completely lost control, and all I knew was to call on God with all my might and in sincerity and in truth.

As I was praying, I could hear the doctors saying, "We got him back." I could not do anything but praise God right there in the hospital. I praise God's Holy name. My father was back. The Power of Prayer is undeniable.

I am a living witness that God answers prayers. I have many testimonies of God answering prayers. God is a prayer answering God. Just try Him!!!!

Another testimony I want to share relates to a very dear friend of mine who was diagnosed with lung cancer. Just to reveal the severity of the illness, she was taken to the emergency room. While being treated, she was told by a doctor in the emergency room that she needed to start making plans and arrangements, because things did not look good. Miraculously, she got better and was able to return home from the emergency room. Praise be to God for restoring her good health.

God's Word

This poor man called, and the Lord heard him;
he saved him out of all his troubles.
~ Psalm 34:16

After being sick for approximately one full year, she went to receive her test results from her doctor's office. While sitting there, the doctor looked at her and then looked back at the results on the report and said to her, "The tumor has shrunk. What happened?" She replied, "People all over the world have been praying for me. Praise God!" This is truly the Power of Prayer.

God will heal. God will restore. God will place tumors in remission. My friend's story has become her testimony of the goodness of God when we pray and have faith in God Almighty. Jesus Christ prayed and we certainly must follow His example.

Through prayer, people are healed, marriages are saved, people are brought together, jobs are found, people are transformed, the impossible becomes the possible, and miracles are performed – right before our eyes. God is able to do all things and we can do all things through Christ Jesus who strengthens us, says the Bible. *Trust in the Lord with all your heart; and lean not on your own understanding. Proverbs 3:5.*

There is so much power that comes from prayer. If you do not understand, just try praying. It works!! I challenge you to try prayer because you will see a difference in whatever the situation might be in your life. I insist that you just try praying and see won't God answer your prayer. You will then know that prayer conquered the issue.

God's Word

I cry out to God Most High, to God, who vindicates me.
~ Psalm 57:2

We must understand, also, that our prayer must be in line with God's plan for our lives. God has commanded us to pray, which you can see from the five prayer scriptures in God's Word:

1) Luke 18:1 - "Then Jesus told his disciples a parable to show them that they should always pray and not give up."

2) Psalm 55:17 - Evening, morning, and noon I cry out in distress, and he hears my voice.

3) Mark 11:24 - "Therefore I say unto you, What things soever ye desire, when ye pray, believe that ye receive them, and ye shall have them."

4) Matthew 6:6 - "But when you pray, go into your room and shut the door and pray to your Father who is in secret. And your father who sees in secret will reward you.

5) Romans 8:26 - "Likewise the Spirit helps us in our weakness. For we do not know what to pray for as we ought, but the Spirit himself intercedes for us with groanings too deep for words."

We are so blessed as God's children to have the ability to talk directly with God, our Father. Oh, what a blessing!

Let us pray so that we will be able to place all our cares and all our worries in the hands of God. He will take care of whatever comes

God's Word

Dear friend, I pray that you may enjoy good health and that all may go well with you, even as your soul is getting along well.
~ 3 John 1:2

our way. Just believe in the power of prayer. For God is able and has power over all the earth, over all the world, and universe.

What a blessing it is to be able to talk to God anytime, anywhere, and as often as we would like. God is available whenever and wherever we are. God is always waiting for you to call upon Him. God is ready to hear your issues, and it is a call you can make morning, noon, or night.

You ought to lift your head up high, giving God all the glory and all the praise for we have a wonderful, loving, and precious God in our lives. Stop worrying, stop being fearful, stop being powerless, fall on your knees, and have a little talk with God about your success, your trials, and your tribulations.

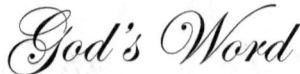

And whenever you stand praying, forgive, if you have anything against anyone, so that your Father also who is in heaven may forgive you your trespasses.
~ Mark 11:25

What Does It Take to Organize a Church Prayer Ministry?

To organize a prayer ministry at your church, you must first realize the power of prayer. Praying as sisters and brothers of the Christian faith is powerful and encouraging. Once you realize the power of prayer, then, you will know the importance of praying privately, praying openly, praying in a group setting, and/or praying as a community.

It is key for church members to know that a praying church body is a powerful body of individuals. This praying body of God's people will make a difference in life through prayer. A praying church becomes stronger in their faith in the Lord because of corporate prayer and praying members. With that being said, we all connect through Jesus' blood. What an awesome family!

God has ordained us to pray as individuals, pray together cooperatively, and work together to win others over to God. Through prayer, we will be able to build God's Kingdom together, and to pray together to glorify God's Holy Name.

In organizing a church prayer ministry, we must know that we gather in prayer to support our sisters and brothers all over the world, because we are one family connected by God. Everyone will be able to say, "There is something special about people who gather together in prayer." People will begin to see the change right before their eyes. People all over the world will be able to say, "They see the God in us" and they will strive to be a part of the body of praying Christians.

When we are connected through Jesus Christ, we praise God together, we worship God together, we support each other together in a time of need, and we walk by faith together. We rejoice with each other together, and we are committed to the trials and tribulations of our sisters and brothers together.

God's Word

They all joined together constantly in prayer, along with the women and Mary the mother of Jesus, and with his brothers.
~ Acts 1:14

Through prayer, all these things are accomplished. As others look on, they will be called to worship God and pray to God for all their needs, and to also thank God for all their blessings.

Now that we are aware that we are all connected as sisters and brothers as one, we must understand that we are privileged to be able to work together in an organized Prayer Ministry through our churches.

In organizing a Prayer Ministry at your church, you would first need to select a sister or brother from the church to organize and lead this ministry – "The Prayer Ministry." This person should be committed to the Lord, have a passion to pray, understand the Word of God, be humble at heart, ready to serve, and willing to serve God's people. They should be willing to invite members, friends, and neighbors to join the Prayer Ministry; and should be dedicated to the goals of the Prayer Ministry – having an eagerness to make the Prayer Ministry a success through fervent prayers.

Just a little talk with God – as a community – will have you able to see the difference right away within the church, within the people, and within the community. A lack of prayer results in people having numerous issues and problems in their home lives, as well as their churches, schools, workplaces, and local communities.

God's Word

When anxiety was great within me,
your consolation brought me joy.
~ Psalm 94:19

Organizing a Church Prayer Ministry

As you prepare and plan how to organize your Prayer Ministry, a special workshop can help kick things off. This workshop should be planned so well that people will *want* to attend, plan, and make recommendations for its success. It would be beneficial to have a workshop at a designated location and time via conference call, Zoom, or in person. At this workshop, make sure all attendees understand the power of prayer and the reason why we need a prayer ministry in each church, create plans for the ministry, and establish the objectives. Allow individuals to volunteer to serve as prayer warriors. As this ministry is established, watch how God impacts the Prayer Ministry and the people.

During the workshop, be sure to gather and share the objectives already established with the group, take the opportunity to make sure everyone understands the planned objectives, share ideas on how to grow the ministry, and utilize the time to get the different groups involved in the Prayer Ministry.

When your team is ready to move forward, do a trial run so everyone will know exactly what to do to begin a successful Prayer Ministry. Be sure to extend an invitation to the members of the church and encourage them to reach out beyond the walls of the church to invite families, neighbors, co-workers, friends, and anyone who is connected to them to join in for prayer.

For the people to connect, they must have a place for the session/meeting, a telephone number (if it is a conference call), or a zoom link (if it is a virtual prayer session). This information should be shared as soon as it has been decided upon. The key objective is to get the people all over the world praying and talking with the Lord, our God.

In organizing a Church Prayer Ministry, there are five important elements you should include to ensure its success:

God's Word

But if serving the LORD seems undesirable to you, then choose for yourselves this day whom you will serve, whether the gods your ancestors served beyond the Euphrates, or the gods of the Amorites, in whose land you are living. But as for me and my household, we will serve the LORD."
~ Joshua 24:15

1) **Organize.**

    a) Select a Leader for the Prayer Ministry that will allow the prayer ministry to strive and flow throughout the entire church.
    b) The selected leader will seek to grow the ministry and as the ministry grows, the leader will be able to break off the one group into additional prayer ministries, according to age, if needed. There can be a Youth Prayer Ministry, Young Adult Prayer Ministry, Adult Prayer Ministry, and a Senior Prayer Ministry. The leader will organize the four different groups and assign prayer warriors to be engaged with the different groups.
    c) The leader should be inclusive of God's people in the Prayer Ministry. All attendees should be encouraged to pray, without judgement of who should be praying to God. God has no respect of persons; therefore, they should follow God's lead and direction for the Prayer Ministry. He will send who and what is needed to advance the Prayer Ministry.

    This is why it's best for the leader to follow God and not their own ideology, as God is in control of all things.

God's Word

Brothers and sisters, choose seven men from among you who are known to be full of the Spirit and wisdom. We will turn this responsibility over to them and will give our attention to prayer and the ministry of the word.
~ Acts 6:3-4

d) Select a name for each individual group Prayer Ministry. Some ideas of great fiery names such as "The Lit Group", "Winds of Fire Group", "Flames of Fire Group", "The Fired- Up Group" and/or "The Tongues of Fire Group."

2) **Gather the Objectives of the Prayer Ministry.**

With the help of your team, formulate the Objectives for the Prayer Ministry at your church.

a) Operate with the prayer objectives in mind.
b) Feel free to add to the objectives or delete, if needed. Add or delete objectives in order to meet the needs of the people. If there is a need to change the objectives, feel free to do so and move the ministry forward.
c) Make sure everyone knows the objectives of the church's Prayer Ministry.
d) Communicate the objectives to everyone.

3) **Teach Your Team the Objectives of the Prayer Ministry.**
Be sure that the team is fully aware of the objectives, understand why they are praying, the importance of praying, and the power of corporate praying.

God's Word

*He will respond to the prayer of the destitute;
he will not despise their plea.*
~ Psalm 102:17

There are six key ingredients to creating an effective prayer session:

a) Give God accolades, glorify God for who God is, and exalt God for all blessings.
b) Praise God for He is worthy to be praised.
c) Thank God for God's blessings.
d) Repent for all sins and seek God always.
e) Tell God what you want.
f) Close the prayer session: In the name of Jesus we pray, Amen.

4) Review what You Have Taught the People.

Make sure that they are all in sync and are ready to receive the Holy Spirit of the Lord's presence.

a) The Leader should review with everyone in attendance and the key leaders for the different groups.
b) Make sure all leaders agree with the objectives and/or edit the objectives for a more comprehensive outcome.
c) Rehearse, if necessary, so no guesswork is needed, and everyone is on the same page.
d) Once all are satisfied, the group is ready and is in sync to move the Prayer Ministry forward.

God's Word

In the morning, Lord, you hear my voice; in the morning I lay my requests before you and wait expectantly.
~ Psalm 5:3

5) Market the Prayer Ministry.

Communicate to other church members, family, and friends, so everyone will feel truly a part of the session with a warm and inviting heart.

a) Share with all the congregational members and friends.
b) State the time and day of each session.
c) Invite people to a join by way of conference-call session, zoom-prayer session, in-person prayer session, and be available for a visit for prayer or a telephone call requesting prayer.
d) Strategically plan a time to tell others about the Prayer Ministry.
e) Use the church's website, announcement boards, social media, and other platforms to make others aware of the Prayer Ministry.

Make sure that the people learn through the marketing process that they can make special requests for prayer according to their needs, or they can share a praise report. Furthermore, make every effort for the people to know of opportunities for individuals to pray online. People can email the team leader and share a prayer request before the session.

God's Word

Yes, and I will continue to rejoice, for I know that through your prayers and God's provision of the Spirit of Jesus Christ what has happened to me will turn out for my deliverance.
~ Philippians 1:19

Invite people to offer up a prayer concern or a praise report for a member of the church, a non-member of the church, and for co-workers, colleagues, friends, and family members. Basically, anyone who wants or needs prayer, please allow their names to be called during the prayer session.

6) Host the Prayer Ministry.

This requires welcoming each person who attends to participate. Start in a timely manner.

a) Be Joyous and happy as we go before the Lord in Prayer.
b) Start promptly.
c) Open with prayer.
d) Share an inspirational message, scripture, or poem.
e) Accept requests for prayer and/or praise reports.
f) Prepare and share a motivational message.
g) End with a closing prayer.

All attendees should be spiritually impacted by the word of God, through the starting prayer, the motivational message, and/or through the closing prayer. You want to be sure to reach each participant during the session through the planned activities.

God's Word

The end of all things is near.
Therefore, be alert and of sober
mind so that you may pray.
~ 1 Peter 4:7

To reach your goal, you must invite, invite, and invite as many people as possible to participate in the Prayer Ministry. Your goal is to get the entire church praying for one another inside and outside the church. Therefore, be inclusive and not exclusive.

God's Word

May the God of hope fill you with all joy and peace as you trust in him, so that you may overflow with hope by the power of the Holy Spirit.
~ Romans 15:13

What is a Prayer Leader?

A prayer leader is an individual who is willing to pray for everyone at any time, for any cause, for any situation, and anywhere.

The prayer leaders is the one who organizes, leads the way for others to follow, and invites other members and friends to join the Prayer Ministry. They should schedule and organize a time for the prayer sessions, encourage the people to participate, facilitate the

Prayer Ministry sessions, welcome everyone who joins, and provide the people with a powerful and effective prayer session – this leads to a church where all ages are involved in praying.

This person or persons are key to the Prayer Ministry, and the Christian Education Director needs them to move the ministry forward successfully. The prayer leader must be compassionate towards others and be willing to listen to the issues presented by the people.

In all that you do, depend on the Holy Spirit to lead you as you pray, in your responses to others, and to direct your path. The Christian Education Director or the leader of the Prayer Ministry should also be prepared to organize, invite people to join, ask for prayer requests, help anyone who needs assistance, and be ready at any time to lead heartfelt and purpose-filled prayers, so the church and the ministry will become a house of prayer.

What are the Characteristics of a Prayer Leader?

There are 10 characteristics of a good Prayer Leader of a church. Those characteristics are listed below:

1. They must love the Lord, our God.
2. They must love God's people.
3. They must be desirous to pray for and help others.

God's Word

In my distress I called to the Lord; I cried to my God for help. From his temple he heard my voice; my cry came before him, into his ears.
~ Psalm 18:6

4. They must be willing to pray for any situation needed.
5. They must be willing to work to expand the ministry through the different organizations in the church.
6. They must be able to retain confidential information given from persons seeking prayer.
7. They must have a good rapport with the pastor, officers, members, and organizational heads.
8. They must possess a humble spirit.
9. They must be sensitive to the needs of others.
10. They should be willing to extend an invitation to all to participate.

God's Word

If you see any brother or sister commit a sin that does not lead to death, you should pray and God will give them life.
~ 1 John 5:16

Summary

Every church must have a Prayer Ministry. If there is no Prayer Ministry, you will have a dead church. As you can see, the Bible does command us to pray, and it tells us about the power of prayer. Therefore, always take advantage of this beautiful gift called prayer. As stated in 1 John 5:14-15,

> *This is the confidence we have in approaching God: that if we ask anything according to his will, he hears us. And if we know that he hears us – whenever we ask – we know that we have what we asked of him.*

God is a prayer-answering God. Remember, God who answers prayer will answer your prayer if it is aligned with God's will for our lives or if it is a part of a plan for our lives.

It is important to remember that God knew us before we ever entered our mother's womb; and, even at that time, God had a plan and a purpose for our lives. We must pray continually until something happens. If our prayers are aligned with the plans of God, they will be answered based on our faith in God. Faith as small as a mustard seed is all we need.

To progress and maintain our stability, we must be dedicated to God in all that we do. God is right in the midst of people who are dedicated to Him and who are willing to obey His commandments. When prayer is the center of our being, God has a unique way of blessing people abundantly through honest and sincere prayers.

As we pray, we want to create life in our church. Prayer brings life to the church, and prayer serves as a lifeline for survival within the church. Without a praying ministry in the church, we cannot move the church forward. God will bring about great changes in the church through prayer, and the people will be able to see the life of the church glow. So, therefore, all people will be able to see the good works of our Father who is in heaven.

The lifelessness of the church reflects a poor prayer life within the church. Every church needs a powerful prayer ministry, a time for devotion with purpose, and an electrifying worship service. As noted by Al Whittinghill, "Without the heartbeat of prayer, the body of Christ will resemble a corpse. The church is dying on her feet because she is not living on her knees."

God's Word

Devote yourselves to prayer,
being watchful and thankful.
~ Colossian 4:2

References

Honorable Mentions:
- Al Whittinghill
  A Teacher and a Preacher; An Ambassador for Christ
- Professor Cynthia Rivers
  The Interdenominational Theological Center
- E. M. Bounds
  A Prayer Hero

Bible Versions:
- Geneva Bible Version (GNV)
- King James Version (KJV)
- New International Version (NIV)
- New Living Translation (NLT)
- New Revised Standard Version (NRSV)

About the Author

Rev. Marilyn Shirelle Burke Udeh was born in Bainbridge, Georgia to Mr. Chester Burke and Mrs. Lillie Mae Burke where she attended a private kindergarten, Hutto Elementary, Middle, and High Schools, and attended Bethune-Cookman University.

After graduating from college, she taught Business Education and Marketing at Washington Street High School in Quitman, Georgia, East High School in Buffalo, New York; Columbia High School and Sequoyah High School in DeKalb County Schools, and Russell/Tri-Cities High School in Fulton County Schools. She is married to Mr. Sunday O. Udeh.

During her marriage, a son was conceived by the name of Alan. He is married to Veronica and they have two daughters named, Amari and Alana.

Rev. Udeh was called into the ministry in 2010 and has not stopped running for the Lord. She thoroughly enjoys teaching, preaching, and serving God and God's people. She was licensed to preach in 2012 by the Atlanta North Georgia Annual Conference Sixth Episcopal District of the African Methodist Episcopal Church and was ordained a Local Deacon on January 11, 2015 and a Local Elder on January 22, 2017.

Her educational background encompasses the following: A Bachelor of Science (BS) Degree in Business Education from Bethune-Cookman University, a Master (MBE) Degree in Business Education from Georgia State University, a second advanced degree – an Education Specialist (Ed.S) in Business and Marketing from Georgia State University; and a Master of Divinity Degree with a concentration in Christian Education from ITC where she graduated with honors on May 9, 2015.

She worked for the school system for over 40 years before retiring from the Fulton County Public Schools as a Marketing Education Coordinator and Partners in Education Coordinator. She enjoyed every single moment of her work experience. After retiring, she was hired back at the same school for another nine years as a Business Partners Coordinator and Parent Liaison. With God right by her side, she enjoyed having great leaders throughout her professional career.

Other Experiences included: Bank Teller-Western Savings Bank-Philadelphia, Adjunct Professor at Clayton State

University and Spelman College; Director of Christian Education at Trinity AME Church; Retooling Facilitator for the South Atlanta District AME Church; Secretary for the Student Christian League at ITC; Treasurer for Theta Phi International Honor Society at ITC; Interned as a Chaplain at WellStar Hospital; Head Chaplain for the Atlanta Suburban Chapter of Delta Sigma Theta Sorority; and Christian Education Director for the South Atlanta District (January 2020).

For over 48 years, she has been a member of Trinity AME Church, assistant pastor for six years (2015), Courtesy Guild president for over 25 years, a member of Delta Sigma Theta Sorority for over 50 years, a member of Theta Phi International Honors Society, and Co-President of the South Fulton Retired Teachers Association for four consecutive years.

She received the following awards and recognitions: Georgia Association of Partners In Education -Partnership of the Year, one of the First Industry Certified Marketing Programs in the Fulton County Schools, Innovative Marketing Teacher of the Year for the State of Georgia, Marketing Education Teacher of the Year for the State of Georgia, Junior Achievement State Teacher of the Year, Russell/Tri-Cities High School Teacher of the Year, Fulton County Schools Recognized her as an Outstanding Teacher, National Association of Blacks in Criminal Justice Community Service Award, Featured in several local and state newspapers, Featured on Channel 11 "Class Notes" for her outstanding accomplishments, Presenter at the local state, and National Marketing Education Conventions, received a Proclamation from the City of East Point, Georgia, and Chaired programs and activities at Trinity AME Church.

THE SOLID FOUNDATION GROUP

Other Books to Enjoy:
www.TheSolidFoundationGroup.com

CHILDREN'S	**THE PIG WHO BECAME PRESIDENT** A Story About Courage and Friendship by Alana Johnson
	SET FREE BY TRUTH by Amari Johnson
	THE ADVENTURES OF NINA SOPHIA Book 1 – Introducing My Big Family by Shatanese Reese and Nina Sophia
	THE ADVENTURES OF NINA SOPHIA Book 2 – My Name is Nina Sophia by Shatanese Reese and Nina Sophia
AUTOBIOGRAPHY / INSPIRATIONAL SELF HELP	**BULLET PROOF** by Bodie Quinette
	A PORTRAIT OF VIRGINIA A. SMITH Gaining Strength Through Life's Journey by Virginia A. Smith
	LIVE EVERY MOMENT My Life as a Super Extra Ordinary Mom by Shatanese Reese
	COLLECT BEAUTIFUL MOMENTS Faith-Based Guided Journal by Shatanese Reese
RELIGION / SPIRITUALITY	**BOUNTIFUL BLESSINGS** 31 Day Devotional by DeAngela S. Reid
	MAN OF VALOR 31 Day Devotional by DeAngela S. Reid

INSTRUCTIONAL	**HOW TO FADE LIKE GRIFFIN** **Barbercation for Today's Barber** by Kendrick Henderson
	CREATING A POWERFUL PRAYER MINISTRY… **Every Church Needs a Prayer Ministry** by Rev. Marilyn Burke Udeh
POETRY	**POETIC MOTIFS' SIGNIFICANCE OF 9** **An Account of Transitional Honesty** by Kish Andes
FICTION / URBAN	**THE CARTEL'S DAUGHTER UNEDITED** by D. D. Carmine
	CHECKMATE **It's Your Move** by Lex
	PIECES OF HER LIFE by G.C. Tindley

All are Available in Print and/or E-Book Formats
Anywhere Books Are Sold.

Google Play

To learn more about the authors and/or their upcoming books |or| to obtain information about becoming an author yourself, please visit our website:

www.TheSolidFoundationGroup.com

www.ingramcontent.com/pod-product-compliance
Lightning Source LLC
Chambersburg PA
CBHW071907070526
44583CB00016B/1881